PAULO COELHO

ENCOUNTERS

2021

Vintage International

Vintage Books
A Division of Penguin Random House LLC
New York

© Paul Macleod

ENCOUNTERS

One day, everything will make sense. Meanwhile,
laugh at all the confusion and weep a little. And know
that everything happens for a reason.

WORDS SPOKEN IN AN INTERVIEW

2021

JANUARY

	S	M	T	W	T	F	S
53						1	2
1	**3**	4	5	6	7	8	9
2	**10**	11	12	13	14	15	16
3	**17**	**18**	19	20	21	22	23
4	**24**	25	26	27	28	29	30
5	**31**						

FEBRUARY

	S	M	T	W	T	F	S
5		1	2	3	4	5	6
6	**7**	8	9	10	11	12	13
7	**14**	15	16	**17**	18	19	20
8	**21**	22	23	24	25	26	27
9	**28**						

MARCH

	S	M	T	W	T	F	S
9		1	2	3	4	5	6
10	**7**	8	9	10	11	12	13
11	**14**	15	16	17	18	19	20
12	**21**	22	23	24	25	26	27
13	**28**	29	30	31			

APRIL

	S	M	T	W	T	F	S
13					1	**2**	3
14	**4**	**5**	6	7	8	9	10
15	**11**	12	13	14	15	16	17
16	**18**	19	20	21	22	23	24
17	**25**	26	27	28	29	30	

MAY

	S	M	T	W	T	F	S
17							1
18	**2**	3	4	5	6	7	8
19	**9**	10	11	12	13	14	15
20	**16**	17	18	19	20	21	22
21	**23**	24	25	26	27	28	29
22	**30**	31					

JUNE

	S	M	T	W	T	F	S
22			1	2	3	4	5
23	**6**	7	8	9	10	11	12
24	**13**	14	15	16	17	18	19
25	**20**	21	22	23	24	25	26
26	**27**	28	29	30			

JULY

	S	M	T	W	T	F	S
26					1	2	3
27	**4**	5	6	7	8	9	10
28	**11**	12	13	14	15	16	17
29	**18**	19	20	21	22	23	24
30	**25**	26	27	28	29	30	31

AUGUST

	S	M	T	W	T	F	S
31	**1**	2	3	4	5	6	7
32	**8**	9	10	11	12	13	14
33	**15**	16	17	18	19	20	21
34	**22**	23	24	25	26	27	28
35	**29**	30	31				

SEPTEMBER

	S	M	T	W	T	F	S
35				1	2	3	4
36	**5**	**6**	7	8	9	10	11
37	**12**	13	14	15	16	17	18
38	**19**	20	21	22	23	24	25
39	**26**	27	28	29	30		

OCTOBER

	S	M	T	W	T	F	S
39						1	2
40	**3**	4	5	6	7	8	9
41	**10**	11	**12**	13	14	15	16
42	**17**	18	19	20	21	22	23
43	**24**	25	26	27	28	29	30
44	**31**						

NOVEMBER

	S	M	T	W	T	F	S
44		1	2	3	4	5	6
45	**7**	8	9	10	11	12	13
46	**14**	15	16	17	18	19	20
47	**21**	22	23	24	**25**	26	27
48	**28**	29	30				

DECEMBER

	S	M	T	W	T	F	S
48				1	2	3	4
49	**5**	6	7	8	9	10	11
50	**12**	13	14	15	16	17	18
51	**19**	20	21	22	23	24	25
52	**26**	27	28	29	30	31	

2022

JANUARY

	S	M	T	W	T	F	S
52							**1**
1	**2**	3	4	5	**6**	7	8
2	**9**	10	11	12	13	14	15
3	**16**	**17**	18	19	20	21	22
4	**23**	24	25	26	27	28	29
5	**30**	31					

FEBRUARY

	S	M	T	W	T	F	S
5			**1**	2	3	4	5
6	**6**	7	8	9	10	11	12
7	**13**	**14**	15	16	17	18	19
8	**20**	**21**	22	23	24	25	26
9	**27**	28					

MARCH

	S	M	T	W	T	F	S
9			**1**	2	3	4	5
10	**6**	7	8	9	10	11	12
11	**13**	14	15	16	17	18	19
12	**20**	21	22	23	24	25	26
13	**27**	28	29	30	31		

APRIL

	S	M	T	W	T	F	S
13						1	2
14	**3**	4	5	6	7	8	9
15	**10**	11	12	13	14	**15**	16
16	**17**	**18**	19	20	21	22	23
17	**24**	25	26	27	28	29	30

MAY

	S	M	T	W	T	F	S
18	**1**	2	3	4	5	6	7
19	**8**	9	10	11	12	13	14
20	**15**	16	17	18	19	20	21
21	**22**	23	24	25	26	27	28
22	**29**	**30**	31				

JUNE

	S	M	T	W	T	F	S
22				1	2	3	4
23	**5**	6	7	8	9	10	11
24	**12**	13	14	15	16	17	18
25	**19**	20	21	22	23	24	25
26	**26**	27	28	29	30		

JULY

	S	M	T	W	T	F	S
26						1	2
27	**3**	**4**	5	6	7	8	9
28	**10**	11	12	13	14	15	16
29	**17**	18	19	20	21	22	23
30	**24**	25	26	27	28	29	30
31	**31**						

AUGUST

	S	M	T	W	T	F	S
31		1	2	3	4	5	6
32	**7**	8	9	10	11	12	13
33	**14**	15	16	17	18	19	20
34	**21**	22	23	24	25	26	27
35	**28**	29	30	31			

SEPTEMBER

	S	M	T	W	T	F	S
35					1	2	3
36	**4**	**5**	6	7	8	9	10
37	**11**	12	13	14	15	16	17
38	**18**	19	20	21	22	23	24
39	**25**	26	27	28	29	30	

OCTOBER

	S	M	T	W	T	F	S
39							1
40	**2**	3	4	5	6	7	8
41	**9**	**10**	11	12	13	14	15
42	**16**	17	18	19	20	21	22
43	**23**	24	25	26	27	28	29
44	**30**	31					

NOVEMBER

	S	M	T	W	T	F	S
44			1	2	3	4	5
45	**6**	7	8	9	10	11	12
46	**13**	14	15	16	17	18	19
47	**20**	21	22	23	**24**	25	26
48	**27**	28	29	30			

DECEMBER

	S	M	T	W	T	F	S
48					1	2	3
49	**4**	5	**6**	7	**8**	9	10
50	**11**	12	13	14	15	16	17
51	**18**	19	20	21	22	23	24
52	**25**	26	27	28	29	30	31

JANUARY 2021

	S	M	T	W	T	F	S
53						**1**	2
1	**3**	4	5	◑	7	8	9
2	**10**	11	12	●	14	15	16
3	**17**	**18**	19	◐	21	22	23
4	**24**	25	26	27	○	29	30
5	**31**						

1 New Year's Day
18 Martin Luther King, Jr. Day

FEBRUARY 2021

	S	M	T	W	T	F	S
5		1	2	3	◑	5	6
6	**7**	8	9	10	●	12	13
7	**14**	**15**	16	17	18	◐	20
8	**21**	22	23	24	25	26	○
9	**28**						

14 Valentine's Day
15 President's Day

MARCH 2021

	S	M	T	W	T	F	S
9		1	2	3	4	5	◑
10	**7**	8	9	10	11	12	●
11	**14**	15	16	17	18	19	20
12	◐	22	23	24	25	26	27
13	○	29	30	31			

APRIL 2021

	S	M	T	W	T	F	S
13					1	**2**	3
14	◐	**5**	6	7	8	9	10
15	**11**	●	13	14	15	16	17
16	**18**	19	◐	21	22	23	24
17	**25**	26	○	28	29	30	

2 **Good Friday**
4 **Easter Sunday**
5 **Easter Monday**

MAY 2021

	S	M	T	W	T	F	S
17							1
18	**2**	◑	4	5	6	7	8
19	**9**	10	●	12	13	14	15
20	**16**	17	18	◐	20	21	22
21	**23**	24	25	○	27	28	29
22	**30**	**31**					

9   **Mother's Day**
31 **Memorial Day**

JUNE 2021

	S	M	T	W	T	F	S
22			1	◑	3	4	5
23	**6**	7	8	9	●	11	12
24	**13**	14	15	16	17	◑	19
25	**20**	21	22	23	○	25	26
26	**27**	28	29	30			

20 **Father's day**

JULY 2021

	S	M	T	W	T	F	S
26					◐	2	3
27	**4**	5	6	7	8	9	●
28	**11**	12	13	14	15	16	◑
29	**18**	19	20	21	22	23	○
30	**25**	26	27	28	29	30	◐

4   **Independence Day**

AUGUST 2021

	S	M	T	W	T	F	S
31	**1**	2	3	4	5	6	7
32	●	9	10	11	12	13	14
33	◑	16	17	18	19	20	21
34	○	23	24	25	26	27	28
35	**29**	◐	31				

SEPTEMBER 2021

	S	M	T	W	T	F	S
35				1	2	3	4
36	**5**	**6**	●	8	9	10	11
37	**12**	◐	14	15	16	17	18
38	**19**	20	○	22	23	24	25
39	**26**	27	28	◑	30		

6   Labor Day

....
....
....
....
....
....
....

OCTOBER 2021

	S	M	T	W	T	F	S
39						1	2
40	**3**	4	5	●	7	8	9
41	**10**	11	**12**	◐	14	15	16
42	**17**	18	19	○	21	22	23
43	**24**	25	26	27	◑	29	30
44	**31**						

12   Columbus Day

....
....
....
....
....
....
....

NOVEMBER 2021

	S	M	T	W	T	F	S
44		1	2	3	●	5	6
45	**7**	8	9	10	◑	12	13
46	**14**	15	16	17	18	○	20
47	**21**	22	23	24	**25**	26	◐
48	**28**	29	30				

11 **Veteran's Day**
25 **Thanksgiving Day**

DECEMBER 2021

	S	M	T	W	T	F	S
48				1	2	3	●
49	**5**	6	7	8	9	10	◑
50	**12**	13	14	15	16	17	18
51	○	20	21	22	23	24	**25**
52	**26**	◐	28	29	30	31	

25 **Christmas Day**

JANUARY

Flexible

Running away from a battle is the worst thing we can do, it's worse than losing a battle, because we can always learn something from defeat, but by running away, all we do is declare victory for our enemy. .

DIARY OF A MAGUS

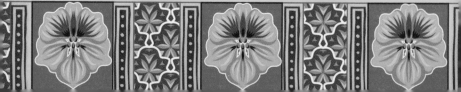

1 Friday

2 Saturday

In the cycle of nature there is no such thing as
victory or defeat; there is only movement.

MANUSCRIPT FOUND IN ACCRA

3 | Sunday

4 | Monday

5 | Tuesday

6 Wednesday

7 Thursday

What is transient?
The inevitable.
What is definitive?
The lessons learned from the inevitable.

THE FIFTH MOUNTAIN

8 Friday

9 Saturday

When a sense of dissatisfaction persists,
that means it was placed there by God for one
reason only: you need to change everything
and move forward.

ALEPH

10 | Sunday

11 | Monday

12 | Tuesday

13 Wednesday

14 Thursday

I don't know if love appears suddenly,
but I do know that I'm open to love, ready for love.

BRIDA

15 Friday

16 Saturday

I don't know if love appears suddenly,
but I do know that I'm open to love, ready for love.

BY THE RIVER PIEDRA I SAT DOWN AND WEPT

17 Sunday

18 Monday

19 Tuesday

20 Wednesday

21 Thursday

Things that don't end clearly always leave a door
open, an unexplored possibility, a chance that
everything might still go back to being
as it was before.

ADULTERY

22 Friday

23 Saturday

It's one thing for the entire universe
to conspire to help us realize our dreams; it's quite
another to place oneself in front of absurd,
unnecessary challenges.

CHRONICLE – THE BLIND MAN AND EVEREST

24 Sunday

25 Monday

26 Tuesday

27 | Wednesday

28 | Thursday

Only someone capable of honoring each step
he takes can comprehend his own worth.

MANUSCRIPT FOUND IN ACCRA

29 Friday

30 Saturday

31 Sunday

Love is the only thing that activates
our intelligence and our creativity,
that purifies and liberates us.

THE ZAHIR

FEBRUARY

Fluid

Life is too short for us to keep important
words locked in our hearts.

MANUSCRIPT FOUND IN ACCRA

1 | Monday

2 | Tuesday

Try to live. Remembering is for the old.

BY THE RIVER PIEDRA I SAT DOWN AND WEPT

3 Wednesday

4 Thursday

5 Friday

6 Saturday

7 Sunday

Only empty hearts can be filled with new things.

CHRONICLE – THE ARRIVAL

8 Monday

9 Tuesday

The word is thought transformed into vibration;
you are projecting into the air around you
something which, before, was only energy.

BRIDA

10 | Wednesday

11 | Thursday

12 Friday

13 Saturday

14 | Sunday

The only trap I must be aware of is thinking that
one day is the same as another.

CHRONICLE – RESPECTING WORK

15 | Monday

16 | Tuesday

There are certain things people should
not ask – if they are not to run away
from their own destiny.

THE ALCHEMIST

17 Wednesday

18 Thursday

19 Friday

20 Saturday

21 | Sunday

In love there is neither good nor evil,
there is neither construction nor destruction,
there is merely movement. And love
changes the laws of nature.

THE ZAHIR

22 Monday

23 Tuesday

Life is not a long vacation,
but a constant learning process.

ADULTERY

24 Wednesday

25 Thursday

26 Friday

27 Saturday

28 Sunday

I believe in having the courage to dream and
paying the price of one's dreams.

CHRONICLE – REPUTATION, INTRIGUES AND LONELINESS

MARCH

Joy

Having a little confidence in life does
no harm, on the contrary, it will allow you
to experience everything much more
intensely.

**CHRONICLE -   FAITH IN LIFE
AND WHAT WILL COME**

1 Monday

2 Tuesday

The greatest manifestation
of the miracle of God is life.

MANUSCRIPT FOUND IN ACCRA

3 Wednesday

4 Thursday

5 Friday

6 Saturday

7 | Sunday

You can't say to the Spring: 'Come now
and last as long as possible.' You can only say:
'Come and bless me with your hope,
and stay as long as you can.'

ELEVEN MINUTES

8 Monday

9 Tuesday

Enthusiasm means trance,
rapture, connection with God.

DIARY OF A MAGUS

10 Wednesday

11 Thursday

12 Friday

13 Saturday

14 Sunday

Love is enough to justify
a whole existence.

THE WITCH OF PORTOBELLO

15 | Monday

16 | Tuesday

I discovered that the search can be as interesting
as actually finding what you're looking for.
As long as you can overcome your fear.

BRIDA

17 Wednesday

18 Thursday

19 Friday

20 Saturday

21 | Sunday

There is nothing sinful about being happy.

DIARY OF A MAGUS

22 Monday

23 Tuesday

What is the meeting?
A way of recovering love.

THE ZAHIR

24 | Wednesday

25 | Thursday

26 Friday

27 Saturday

28 | Sunday

When we search for love with courage,
it reveals itself, and we end up
attracting more love.

BY THE RIVER PIEDRA I SAT DOWN AND WEPT

29 | Monday

30 | Tuesday

I have two ways of showing my love of God:
the first is to praise Him day and night...
The second is to sing, dance, and show His face
to all through my joy.

HIPPIE

31 Wednesday

APRIL

Empathy

The dunes change with the wind,
but the desert remains the same.
That is how our love will be.

THE ALCHEMIST

1 | Thursday

Have pity on those who gave everything
and are charitable and try to overcome
evil with love alone.

DIARY OF A MAGUS

2 Friday

3 Saturday

To keep love locked inside us is to go against
the spirit of God, it is proof that we never
knew Him, that He loved us in vain.

SPEECH AT THE BRAZILIAN ACADEMY OF LETTERS

4 | Sunday

5 | Monday

6 | Tuesday

7 Wednesday

8 Thursday

It's easy to suffer for the love of a particular
cause or mission; this only makes the heart
of the person suffering bigger.

BY THE RIVER PIEDRA I SAT DOWN AND WEPT

9 Friday

10 Saturday

Love is patient.

ADULTERY

11 | Sunday

12 | Monday

13 | Tuesday

14 Wednesday

15 Thursday

We are not the judges or critics of the dreams of others. In order to have faith in our own path, we do not need to prove that other people's paths are wrong.

MAKTUB – AN END TO PREJUDICE

16 Friday

17 Saturday

Anyone who tries to possess a flower will have
to watch its beauty fading. But if you simply look
at a flower in a field, you will keep it forever.

B R I D A

18 | Sunday

19 | Monday

20 | Tuesday

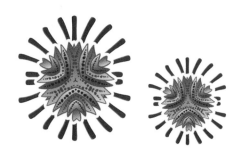

21 | Wednesday

22 | Thursday

Love is an act of faith in another person and their
face should remain wrapped in mystery.

CHRONICLE – REGARDING MYSTERY

23 | Friday

---

24 | Saturday

Love arrives, moves in and starts directing
everything. Only very strong souls allow
themselves to be swept along.

THE WITCH OF PORTOBELLO

25 Sunday

26 Monday

27 Tuesday

28 Wednesday

29 Thursday

Love arrives, moves in and starts directing
everything. Only very strong souls allow
themselves to be swept along.

THE WITCH OF PORTOBELLO

30 | Friday

Do not fight in order to prove that you are right
or to impose your ideas or ideals on someone
else. Accept the fight only as a way of keeping
your spirit clean and your will spotless.

MANUSCRIPT FOUND IN ACCRA

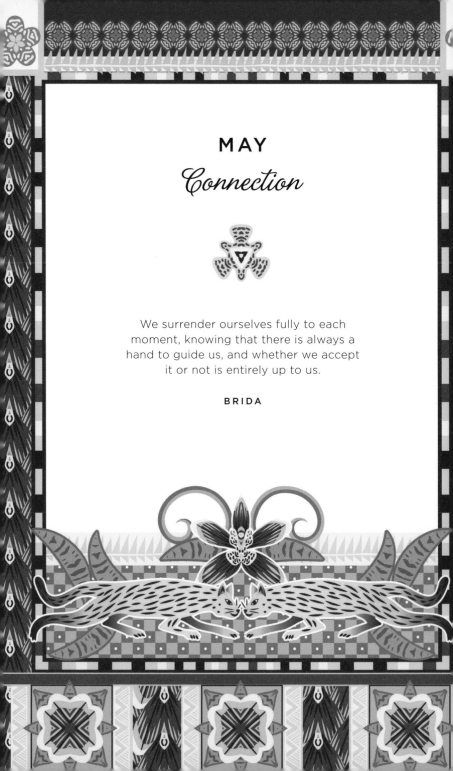

MAY

Connection

We surrender ourselves fully to each
moment, knowing that there is always a
hand to guide us, and whether we accept
it or not is entirely up to us.

BRIDA

1 | Saturday

2 Sunday

It is in the realm of Love
that we fight our first battles.

MANUSCRIPT FOUND IN ACCRA

3 Monday

4 Tuesday

They were all looking for meaning
in their lives, but while they were looking,
they were able to transform their steps into
manifestations of love for their fellow
men and women.

SPEECH AT THE BRAZILIAN ACADEMY OF LETTERS

5 Wednesday

6 Thursday

7 | Friday

8 | Saturday

9 Sunday

The messsenger helps, but there
is something that exists beyond the domain
of the messenger, your desires and yourself.
What's that?
The divine spark. What people call chance.

DIARY OF A MAGUS

10 | Monday

---

11 | Tuesday

A warrior of light shares
his world with those he loves.

MANUAL OF THE WARRIOR OF LIGHT

12 | Wednesday

13 | Thursday

14 Friday

15 Saturday

16 | Sunday

You may find solitude oppressive,
too much to bear, but that feeling
will gradually disappear as you come more
into contact with other people.

ALEPH

17 Monday

18 Tuesday

A love that owes nothing to anyone,
that has no obligations, that finds joy in the simple
existence and the freedom to express itself.

HIPPIE

19 | Wednesday

20 | Thursday

21 Friday

22 Saturday

23 Sunday

God does not play dice with the Universe,
everything is interconnected and has a meaning.

THE ZAHIR

24 Monday

25 Tuesday

There may well be quicker or easier methods,
that doesn't matter; what matters
is that the Tradition remains unchanged.

BRIDA

26 Wednesday

27 Thursday

28 Friday

29 Saturday

30 | Sunday

The miracle is something that suddenly
fills our hearts with Love. When that happens,
we feel a profound reverence for the grace
God has bestowed on us.

MANUSCRIPT FOUND IN ACCRA

31 | Monday

Everyone has the authority
of an official when he or she is absolutely
convinced of what he or she is doing.

LIKE THE RIVER THAT FLOWS

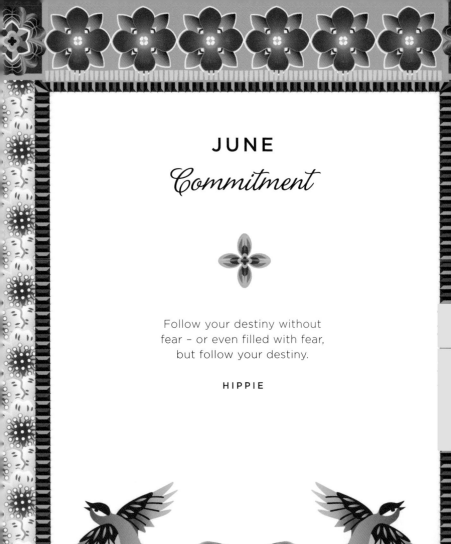

JUNE

Commitment

Follow your destiny without
fear – or even filled with fear,
but follow your destiny.

HIPPIE

---

1 | Tuesday

The worst thing isn't to fall,
it's to stay there, lying on the ground.

MANUSCRIPT FOUND IN ACCRA

2 Wednesday

3 Thursday

4 | Friday

5 | Saturday

6 Sunday

It's never too late to live your dreams.

FROM A CHRONICLE – BEGINNING AT 70

7 Monday

8 Tuesday

A warrior of light
does not postpone making decisions.

MANUAL OF THE WARRIOR OF LIGHT

9 Wednesday

_____

10 Thursday

_____

11 Friday

12 Saturday

13 | Sunday

Once we have chosen our path,
let us never look back and never allow our soul
to be eaten away by remorse.

CHRONICLE – THE PRAYER I FORGOT

14 Monday

15 Tuesday

Life loses its meaning
when the building stops.

BRIDA

16 Wednesday

17 Thursday

18 Friday

19 Saturday

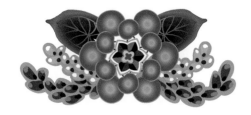

20 Sunday

History is full of legends about heroes
and heroines, not stories about the vanquishers
or the vanquished, but about people who travel
the world, contemplate the steppes, and allow
themselves to be filled by the energy of love.

THE ZAHIR

21 Monday

22 Tuesday

When every day seems the same,
that's because people have stopped noticing
the good things that appear in their lives
whenever the sun crosses the sky.

THE ALCHEMIST

23 | Wednesday

24 | Thursday

25 Friday

26 Saturday

27 Sunday

I wish I had no control over my heart.

BY THE RIVER PIEDRA I SAT DOWN AND WEPT

28 Monday

29 Tuesday

A warrior on the battlefield is fulfilling his destiny,
and he must surrender himself to that.

MANUSCRIPT FOUND IN ACCRA

30 | Wednesday

JULY

Support

Luck is knowing to look around you
and see where your friends are, because
it's through their words that the angels are
able to make themselves heard.

THE ZAHIR

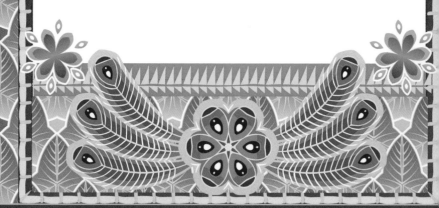

1 Thursday

Love is only a word, until someone
arrives to give it meaning.

MANUSCRIPT FOUND IN ACCRA

2 | Friday

3 | Saturday

However intelligent a man may be, he will soon
lose his warmth and his flame if he distances
himself from his fellow man.

LIKE THE FLOWING RIVER

4 | Sunday

5 Monday

6 Tuesday

7 Wednesday

8 Thursday

Love is understood to be something
much larger than the simple act of liking.

SPEECH AT THE BRAZILIAN ACADEMY OF LETTERS

9 Friday

10 Saturday

A warrior of light shares with others
what he knows of the path.

MANUAL OF THE WARRIOR OF LIGHT

11 | Sunday

12 Monday

13 Tuesday

14 Wednesday

15 Thursday

Charity is also only one of the many
roads that Love uses to bring man
closer to his fellow man.

ADULTERY

16 Friday

17 Saturday

Anyone who has the courage to say
what he feels in his soul is in touch with God.

CHRONICLE – THE TREE AND ITS FRUITS

18 | Sunday

19 Monday

20 Tuesday

21 Wednesday

22 Thursday

Controlling your aggression
in order not to harm the other
is the Path to Peace.

ALEPH

23 Friday

24 Saturday

We will not fear what happens tomorrow,
because yesterday we had someone
watching over us.

MANUSCRIPT FOUND IN ACCRA

25 | Sunday

26 Monday

27 Tuesday

28 Wednesday

29 Thursday

The warrior of light pays attention
to small things because they can
severely hamper him.

MANUAL OF THE WARRIOR OF LIGHT

30 Friday

31 Saturday

To fight is not a sin.
To fight is an act of love.

DIARY OF A MAGUS

AUGUST

Union

A warrior of light knows that
no man is an island.

MANUAL OF THE WARRIOR OF LIGHT

The moment we set off in search of love,
love sets out to meet us.

BY THE RIVER PIEDRA I SAT DOWN AND WEPT

1 | Sunday

2 Monday

3 Tuesday

4 Wednesday

5 Thursday

Stay close to those who are by your side in happy
times, because they do not harbor jealousy or
envy in their hearts, only joy to see you happy.

MANUSCRIPT FOUND IN ACCRA

6 Friday

7 Saturday

A man who cannot hear, cannot
hear the advice that life gives us at every moment.

DIARY OF A MAGUS

8 Sunday

9 Monday

10 Tuesday

11 Wednesday

12 Thursday

Although thoughts always remain the same,
there is something stronger, and this is called
Love. Because when we truly love, we know
others and ourselves better.

THE SPY

13 Friday

14 Saturday

People have been searching for and finding each
other for thousands of years.

BRIDA

15 | Sunday

16 Monday

17 Tuesday

18 Wednesday

19 Thursday

It is our wings that allow
us to know the roots of our fellow human
beings and to learn with them.

THE WINNER STANDS ALONE

20 Friday

21 Saturday

The final test of any search is the size
and extent of our love and what we do or believe
or achieve will count for nothing.

SPEECH AT THE BRAZILIAN ACADEMY OF LETTERS

22 | Sunday

23 Monday

24 Tuesday

25 | Wednesday

26 | Thursday

Just as there are many paths to the top
of a mountain, so there are many paths
to achieving our goal. Help us to recognize
the only one that is worth following:
the one on which Love is to be found.

MANUSCRIPT FOUND IN ACCRA

27 | Friday

28 | Saturday

The man who keeps his friends
is never overwhelmed by the storms of life;
he is strong enough to come through
difficulties and to carry on.

MANUAL OF THE WARRIOR OF LIGHT

29 | Sunday

30 Monday

31 Tuesday

Loyalty can never be imposed by force,
fear, insecurity or intimidation.

MANUCRIPT FOUND IN ACCRA

SEPTEMBER

Fidelity

In the love of a woman,
I discovered a love for all creatures.

THE FIFTH MOUNTAIN

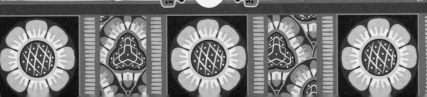

1 Wednesday

2 Thursday

I am a slave only to my heart, and in that case,
my burden is a very light one.

THE WINNER STANDS ALONE

3 Friday

4 Saturday

5 Sunday

The greatest gift God gave us
is the power to make decisions.

MANUSCRIPT FOUND IN ACCRA

6 Monday

7 Tuesday

The gates of Paradise would
be open to anyone determined to enter them.

THE VALKYRIES

8 Wednesday

9 Thursday

10 Friday

11 Saturday

12 Sunday

The path often contradicts itself in order
to encourage the traveller to discover
what lies around the next bend.

**CHRONICLE – BETWEEN EKATERINBURG
AND NOVOSIBIRSK**

13 Monday

14 Tuesday

The true companions of a warrior
are beside him always, during the difficult
times and the easy times.

MANUAL OF THE WARRIOR OF LIGHT

15 Wednesday

16 Thursday

17 Friday

18 Saturday

19 Sunday

Suffering occurs when we want other people
to love us in the way we imagine we want to be
loved, and not in the way that love should
manifest itself.

THE ZAHIR

20 Monday

21 Tuesday

Anyone who loves has to learn how to lose
himself and to find himself.

BY THE RIVER PIEDRA I SAT DOWN AND WEPT

22 Wednesday

23 Thursday

24 Friday

25 Saturday

26 Sunday

God wrote on the world which path each
man should follow, it's just a matter of reading
what He wrote for you.

THE ALCHEMIST

27 Monday

28 Tuesday

Fight to fulfil your destiny, and give no thought
to profits or advantages, losses or strategies,
victories or defeats.

HIPPIE

29 Wednesday

30 Thursday

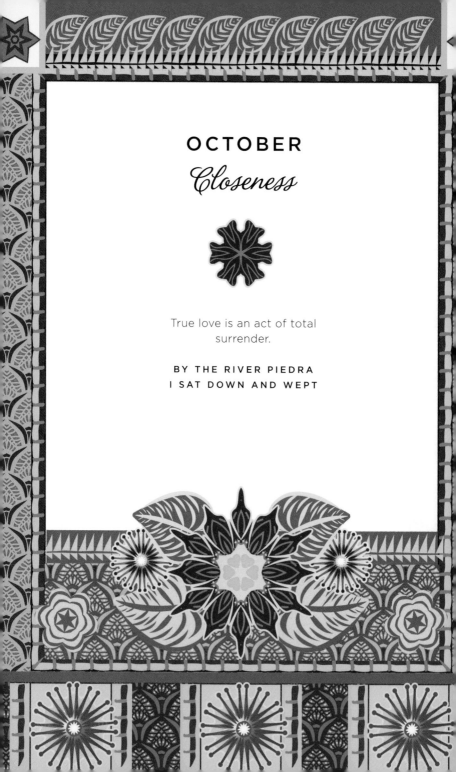

OCTOBER

Closeness

True love is an act of total
surrender.

**BY THE RIVER PIEDRA
I SAT DOWN AND WEPT**

1 Friday

2 Saturday

It is better to have loved and lost than never
to have loved at all.

MANUSCRIPT FOUND IN ACCRA

3 | Sunday

4 Monday

5 Tuesday

6 Wednesday

7 Thursday

Whenever you want to achieve something,
keep your eyes wide open, concentrate
and know exactly what you want.

THE DEVIL AND MISS PRYM

8 Friday

9 Saturday

The prime virtue of those seeking
the spiritual path is courage.

THE VALKYRIES

10 | Sunday

11 | Monday

12 | Tuesday

13 Wednesday

14 Thursday

There are still times when
it is necessary to take risks.

BY THE RIVER PIEDRA I SAT DOWN AND WEPT

15 Friday

16 Saturday

We can make many mistakes in our life,
except one, the one that destroys us.

VERONIKA DECIDES TO DIE

17 | Sunday

18 Monday

19 Tuesday

20 | Wednesday

21 | Thursday

Only by accepting our desires can we have
some idea of who we are.

BRIDA

22 | Friday

23 | Saturday

I'm not afraid of loneliness... I'm afraid of deluding
myself, of looking at reality the way I would
like it to be and not how it really is.

ADULTERY

24 Sunday

25 | Monday

26 | Tuesday

27 Wednesday

28 Thursday

You need to find the treasure
so that everything you have discovered
on the path can make sense.

THE ALCHEMIST

29 Friday

30 Saturday

That is what marks out the warrior:
the knowledge that will power and courage are
not the same thing. Courage can attract fear and
adulation, but willpower requires patience
and commitment.

ALEPH

31 | Sunday

NOVEMBER

Purpose

Remember your dreams
and fight for them.

TWITTER

1 Monday

2 Tuesday

In this life only do what is worthwhile.
Only then will you understand the great
transformations to come.

THE VALKYRIES

3 Wednesday

4 Thursday

5 Friday

6 Saturday

7 Sunday

'What are you good at?'
'Going after what I believe in.'

BRIDA

8 Monday

9 Tuesday

The warrior of light knows the value
of persistence and courage.

MANUAL OF THE WARRIOR OF LIGHT

10 Wednesday

11 Thursday

12 | Friday

13 | Saturday

14 Sunday

Flee routine and try something new, something
spectacular. That could open the doors to a great
adventure, both human and spiritual.

CHRONICLE – MAKTUB MYSTERIES

15 Monday

16 Tuesday

When you want something, the whole universe
conspires to help you fulfill your desire.

THE ALCHEMIST

17 | Wednesday

18 | Thursday

19 Friday

20 Saturday

21 Sunday

To have courage, you must conquer your fears...
We can't forget that life is on our side. It also
wants to get better.

ADULTERY

22 | Monday

23 | Tuesday

Love never distanced anyone
from his or her dreams.

BY THE RIVER PIEDRA I SAT DOWN AND WEPT

24 | Wednesday

25 | Thursday

26 | Friday

27 | Saturday

It isn't difficult to rebuild a life, just as it's not
impossible to rise up again. We simply have to be
aware that we have the same strength we had
before and use it to our advantage

THE FIFTH MOUNTAIN

28 Sunday

29 Monday

30 Tuesday

Disappointment, defeat and despair
are the tools God uses to show us the way.

BRIDA

DECEMBER

Metamorphosis

If you want to see a rainbow
you have to learn to like the rain.

ALEPH

1 Wednesday

2 Thursday

What is this force that propels us far from all
that is familiar and makes us face challenges, even
though we know how transient worldly glory is?

SPEECH AT THE BRAZILIAN ACADEMY OF LETTERS

3 | Friday

4 | Saturday

5 | Sunday

None of us can know what tomorrow
will hold, because each day has its good
and its bad moments.

MANUSCRIPT FOUND IN ACCRA

6 | Monday

7 | Tuesday

The Path to Peace is the art of filling up
what is missing and emptying out what
is superfluous.

ALEPH

8 | Wednesday

9 | Thursday

10 Friday

11 Saturday

12 Sunday

We study what we can see, but what
we see is not always what exists.

BRIDA

13 Monday

14 Tuesday

We are not alone. The world is constantly
changing and we are part of that change.
The angels guide and protect us.

THE VALKYRIES

15 Wednesday

16 Thursday

17 Friday

18 Saturday

19 Sunday

When I experienced humiliation and
yet kept on walking, I understood that I was free
to choose my destiny.

THE ZAHIR

20 | Monday

21 | Tuesday

Love transforms, love heals.

MANUSCRIPT FOUND IN ACCRA

22 Wednesday

23 Thursday

24 Friday

25 Saturday

26 Sunday

A Yes or a No can change
our whole existence.

BY THE RIVER PIEDRA I SAT DOWN AND WEPT

27 Monday

28 Tuesday

Fear exists until the moment when the inevitable
occurs. After that, we should not waste our
energies on it.

THE FIFTH MOUNTAIN

29 Wednesday

30 Thursday

31 | Friday

All wines should be tasted;
some should only be sipped, but with others,
drink the whole bottle.

BRIDA

Original title: *Encontros 2021*

Copyright © 2020 by Paulo Coelho and Mosaikk AS
http://paulocoelhoblog.com/

All rights reserved. Published in the United States of America by Vintage Books,
a division of Penguin Random House LLC, New York,
and distributed in Canada by Random House of Canada,
a division of Penguin Random House Canada Limited, Toronto.

Published by arrangement with Sant Jordi Asociados, Agencia Literaria, S.L.U.,
Barcelona (Spain). www.santjordi-asociados.com

Vintage is a registered trademark and Vintage International and the colophon
are trademarks of Penguin Random House LLC.

Vintage ISBN: 978-0-593-08297-3

Quote selection: Márcia Botelho
Translation copyright © Margaret Jull Costa
Illustrations by Catalina Estrada, www.catalinaestrada.com
Author photograph © Paul Macleod
Design by Lene Stangebye Geving / Mireia Barreras

www.vintagebooks.com

Printed and bound by TBB, a. s., Slovakia, 2020

First Vintage International edition: August 2020